GREGORY L. VOGT

THE SUN

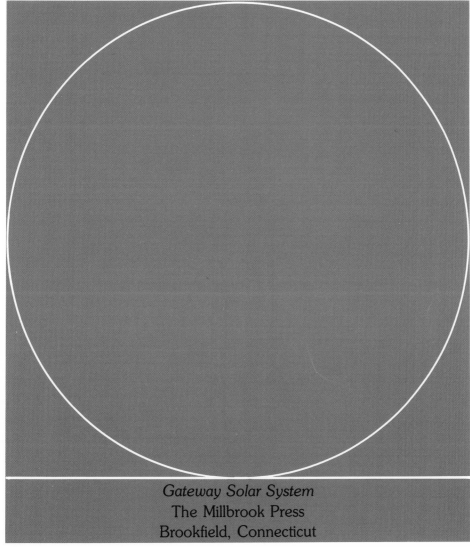

Gateway Solar System
The Millbrook Press
Brookfield, Connecticut

The images of the Sun on the cover and pages 7, 10, and 13 were acquired by the Soft X-ray Telescope on the Yohkoh solar research spacecraft of the Japanese Institute of Space and Astronomical Science. The Soft X-ray Telescope experiment is a Japan/U.S. collaboration involving the National Astronomical Observatory of Japan, the University of Tokyo, and the Lockheed Palo Alto Research Laboratory. The U.S. work is supported by the National Aeronautics and Space Administration.

Cover photograph: The Sun's photosphere or apparent surface was photographed by the Yohkoh satellite on November 12, 1991. The satellite is used to study X-ray radiation emitted by the Sun. Courtesy NASA/Japanese Institute of Space and Astronomical Science.

Photographs courtesy of Greg Vogt: p. 4; NASA/Japanese Institute of Space and Astronomical Science: pp. 7, 10, 13; National Optical Astronomy Observatories: pp. 11 (both), 22, 25; NASA: pp. 12, 14, 15, 17, 19, 20, 21, 24 (Dr. Christopher Burrows, ESA/STscl).

Library of Congress Cataloging-in-Publication Data
Vogt, Gregory.
The sun / Gregory L. Vogt.
p. cm.
Includes bibliographical references and index.
Summary: Presents information on the composition, atmosphere, and origin of the Sun.
ISBN 1-56294-600-5 (Lib. Bdg.)
1. Sun—Juvenile literature. [1. Sun.] I. Title.
QB521.5V64   1996
523.7—dc20   95-19739   CIP   AC

Published by The Millbrook Press, Inc.
2 Old New Milford Road
Brookfield, Connecticut 06804

THE SUN

Some of the Sun's nearest star neighbors look like colorful streaks or "star trails" in this picture. The photographic film was exposed for an hour to capture the faint star light. Because of the Earth's rotation, the stars appear to move across the sky, which creates the trails of light on the film.

Our Sun is not a very big or a very bright star. It is just one star in the huge *Milky Way galaxy,* home to hundreds of billions of stars. Although compared to other stars, our Sun is average, it is very important to us.

The Sun is at the center of a solar system of 9 planets, 63 moons, and trillions of asteroids, comets, and meteors. These planets, moons, and other heavenly bodies are held in place by the Sun's *gravity.* We live in this solar system, on Earth, the third planet from the Sun. Earth receives just the right amount of light and warmth from the Sun to enable us and all living things to survive. If the Sun didn't exist, we wouldn't either.

When we think of stars, we think of thousands of twinkling lights that flash in the clear night sky. Because the Sun is so big and bright and floods our sky with light, we don't think of it as a star. The only real difference between the night stars and the Sun, however, is how far away they are from us.

The Sun looks big and bright to us because it is not very far away. It is only about 93 million miles (150 million kilometers) from Earth. That sounds like a great distance, but compared to the other stars in the sky, the Sun is only a hop, skip, and jump away. The next nearest star to us, Proxima Centauri, is more than 265,000

times as far away! If we could push the Sun deep into space, to where some of the other stars are, we probably wouldn't even be able to see it.

What is the Sun? How big is it? What is it made of? Where does the Sun get all the energy that it sends to Earth and out into space? We know that the Sun is a star, but what are stars?

Stars are glowing balls of gas. Our star, the Sun, is a huge ball, 864,000 miles (1,390,000 kilometers) in diameter. It is so large that if it were empty, you could put 1 million planet Earths inside it. The Sun is also very heavy. If you could put the Sun on one side of a gigantic seesaw, you would need 333,000 Earths on the other side to balance it.

Hot Gases

The Sun is a complicated world of seething hot gases and erupting magnetic storms. It has a gigantic atmosphere and it blows winds of electrically charged particles out beyond the orbit of Pluto, the last planet in the solar system.

There are two main gases that make up the Sun: hydrogen and helium. Hydrogen is one of the elements found in water. Helium is the gas sometimes put into balloons to make them float in air.

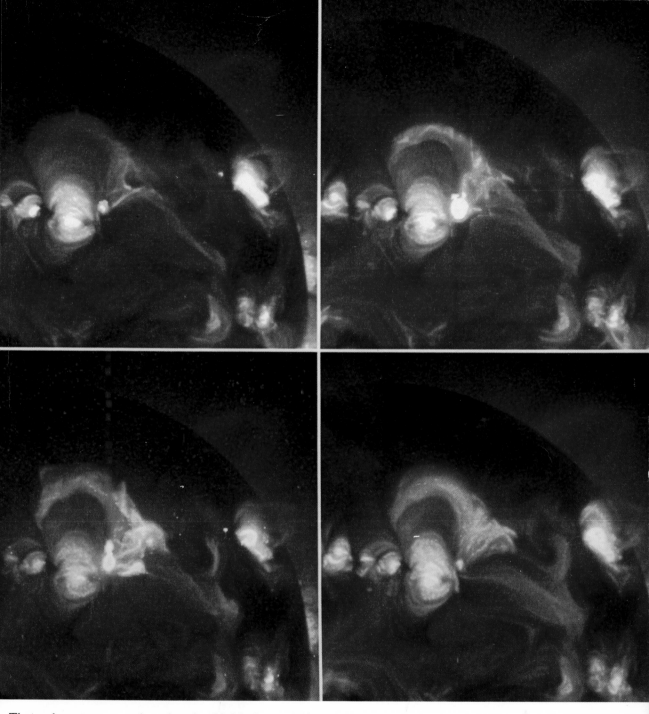

These four images taken by the Yohkoh satellite show close-up details of the Sun's edge. Bright swirling lines show the effects of the Sun's magnetic field on the gases in the Sun's atmosphere.

About 90 percent of the atoms in the Sun are hydrogen atoms. Most of the other 10 percent are helium atoms. Without the pull of the Sun's strong gravity, these gases would escape into space. The Sun's gravity pulls the gases close together, toward the center of the Sun. The gases become very compressed and very hot. At the Sun's center, the temperature reaches more than 27 million degrees Fahrenheit (more than 15 million degrees Celsius). The pressure is so great in the center that the gas is squeezed to a *density* that is more than ten times greater than that of iron.

The combination of high temperatures and great pressures triggers an important reaction called *fusion*. Fusion is the process that makes hydrogen bombs work. When fusion takes place, the Sun's hydrogen atoms join together and become helium atoms. Tremendous amounts of energy are released.

Because the Sun is so dense, that energy can take millions of years to escape beyond the Sun's surface. When it does escape, the energy travels through space as light. In only eight and a half minutes, the energy reaches Earth, where it lights and heats our world. As great as this energy seems to us, it is only a tiny part (about one two-billionth) of all the energy the Sun sends into space!

Even though it is made up of gases, the Sun looks round to us. (Be sure never to stare at the Sun because you can damage your eyes.) The Sun appears to be the same size as a full Moon, even though it is much bigger, because the Sun is a greater distance away from us. It looks white when it is overhead, but sometimes it can look yellowish or very red. This change in color is not due to changes in the Sun, but to the way the sunlight is absorbed by Earth's *atmosphere.* Early in the morning or late in the afternoon, when the Sun is low in the sky, the Earth's atmosphere blocks some of the colors in the sunlight. The color that is left that you see is yellow or red.

If you do glance at the Sun or look at pictures of it taken with *solar telescopes,* the part of the Sun you see is called the *photosphere.* The photosphere is the surface, or skin, of the Sun. It is made up of gases that are about 10,500 degrees Fahrenheit (5,800 degrees Celsius).

When greatly magnified by telescopes, the photosphere looks violent and explosive. Hot material boils up to the surface and spreads outward to form circular pools, or *granules,* 450 to 600 miles (720 to 1,000 kilometers) wide. Because of these granules, the Sun's surface looks grainy when seen through the solar telescope.

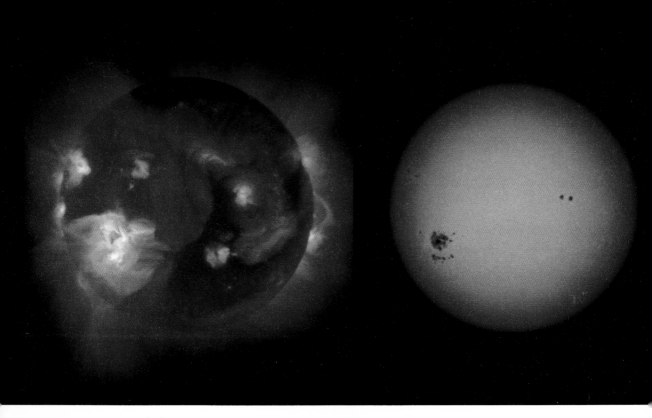

These two pictures taken by the Yohkoh satellite show the Sun in X-ray light (left) and in white light (right), the light our eyes are sensitive to. Several sunspots are visible in the photo at right. The photo at left shows that bright flares occurred in the same areas.

(You can see a similar effect if you watch a pot of soup simmering on a stove.) Within minutes, old granules are replaced by new ones erupting from below. Occasionally, much larger granules form and can last from 12 to 24 hours. These are *supergranules* and may be 19,000 miles (30,600 kilometers) wide.

In some areas of the Sun's surface there are cooler pools of materials. They do not give off as much light as other, hotter areas. Viewed from Earth, these pools appear dark. They are called *sunspots*. Sunspots can be from 600 miles (1,000 kilometers) to tens of thousands of miles wide.

Mysteriously, every 11 years or so, the magnetic activity on the Sun seems to peak. At that time, many more sunspots are visible.

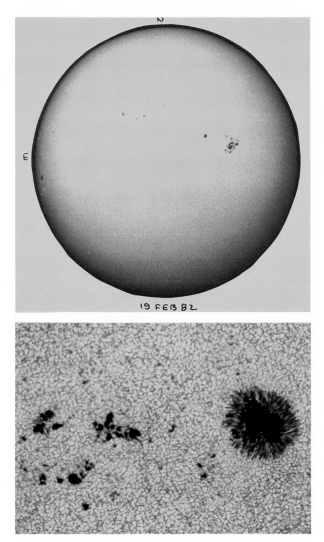

Sunspots are visible in this photo taken on February 19, 1982.

The dark regions in this close-up telescope view of the Sun are sunspots, the cooler areas of the surface. The surrounding, hotter areas look granular.

Even stranger than the sunspots are the *spicules, flares,* and *prominences.* Spicules are spike-shaped storms that blast thousands of miles up into the Sun's atmosphere. Spicules erupt from the gaps between the granules. Flares are powerful explosions that shoot long streams of electrically charged particles into space. Some flares give off as much energy as 10 million hydrogen bombs exploding all at once!

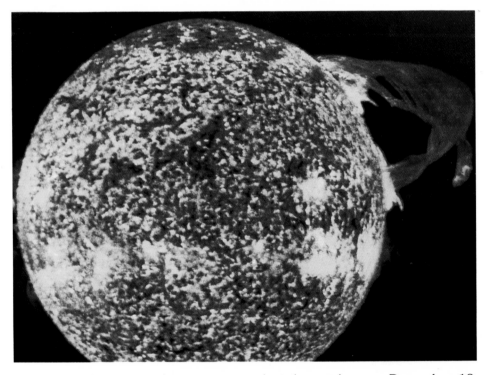

The Sun's churning surface is seen in this photo taken on December 19, 1973, by Skylab astronauts. The huge solar flare, which looks like a twisted sheet of gas, attracted the astronauts' attention. The two ends of the prominence span 365,000 miles (590,000 kilometers) across the solar surface.

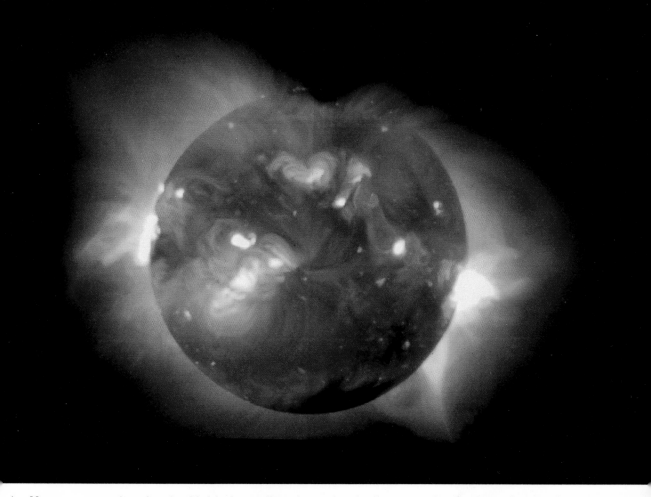

An X-ray image taken by the Yohkoh satellite shows bright flares on the Sun's surface and corona.

The most spectacular events on the Sun are the prominences. Millions of tons of hot, glowing gas are blasted hundreds of thousands of miles upward. The glowing gas forms arch-shaped ribbons in the Sun's atmosphere. The ribbons take their shape from the Sun's magnetic field. (If you have ever sprinkled iron filings over a bar magnet, you will have seen the filings form arching lines around the magnet. Prominences are shaped in similar ways.) Sometimes prominences do not begin with a blast. Instead they form from condensed gases in the atmosphere and fall into the Sun.

The Atmosphere

Every so often, Earth's Moon crosses directly in front of the Sun. If the Sun, Earth, and Moon line up perfectly, the Moon completely covers, or eclipses, the Sun's photosphere. When this happens, something marvelous takes place. The Sun's huge but very dim atmosphere becomes visible.

This total eclipse of the Sun was seen in Miahu-atlan, Mexico, on March 7, 1970. The Moon was directly in front of the Sun for 3½ minutes.

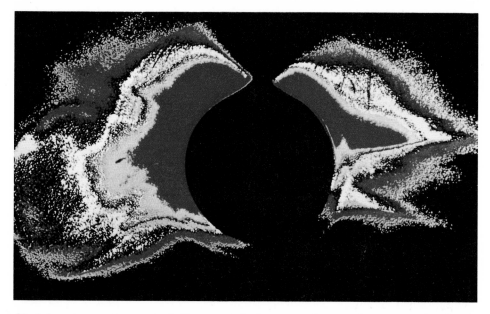

Skylab astronauts created this special photograph in order to see the Sun's corona. They blocked out the brightest part of the Sun and added colors to show the brightness of each of the areas of the Sun's outer atmosphere.

The brightest part of the Sun's atmosphere is a thin, ragged, pinkish rim of gas, about 1,600 miles (2,600 kilometers) deep, surrounding the photosphere. Because it is so colorful, this layer of gas is called the *chromosphere* (which means "color sphere").

Above the chromosphere lies the upper atmosphere, or *corona*. The inner part of the corona is visible during an eclipse and is about as bright as the full Moon. The shape of the inner corona changes. Sometimes it has the appearance of flames; at other times it is fan-shaped.

Beyond the inner corona is the invisible outer corona. Its size varies, but it can extend beyond the orbit of Earth! The outer corona is made up of very thin gases. You could pass right through it and never know it is there.

One of the amazing things about the corona is how hot it is. If you travel from the photosphere of the Sun outward into space, the temperature does the opposite of what you would expect it to do: Instead of falling, it rises. The chromosphere, or lowest layer of the atmosphere, is about five times hotter than the photosphere. The temperature in the corona climbs to millions of degrees! This is one of the Sun's great mysteries that scientists hope to understand someday.

How could you pass through the outer corona, where temperatures range in the millions of degrees, and not feel it? Compare the corona to the air in a hot oven. You can stick your hand inside a hot oven without getting burned, although you can't pick up the bread pan inside without pot holders! The bread pan is dense and contains a lot of heat. The thin air in the oven, although it is at the same high temperature as the bread pan, doesn't contain much heat. The corona also has an extremely low density and doesn't contain much heat.

The solar corona as seen by NASA's Solar Maximum Mission satellite. Colors have been added to the pictures to show the different densities of the corona. Purple is the densest and coolest; yellow is the least dense and hottest in temperature. The pointed structure in the upper right of the photograph is a solar spike, or streamer, that extends millions of miles into space.

Wind from the Sun

Scientists believe that the heat of the Sun's outer corona creates a very low-density *solar wind* of electrically charged gas. The particles race outward through the solar system at speeds from 190 to 440 miles (300 to 700 kilometers) per second.

Although the solar winds cannot be seen, their effects can be. The particles are electrically charged, so they can be trapped in Earth's magnetic field. The presence of solar-wind particles will sometimes trigger the beautiful *auroras,* or northern and southern lights, seen in the night skies. When frozen comets swing near the Sun, the gases they release are blown by the solar wind and form long tails pointing away from the Sun's surface.

The Beginning

Where did the Sun and its solar system come from? What will happen to the Sun in the future? Astronomers have been trying to answer these questions for hundreds of years. Today, they think they have some of the answers, but there is still much to learn, and their ideas change as they continue to make new discoveries.

When the solar wind reaches Earth's atmosphere, its particles react with the thin gases, causing a colorful glow called auroras, or the northern lights and the southern lights. This aurora was photographed by space-shuttle astronauts on the STS-39 mission in 1991.

Scientists continue to gather information about the Sun. In 1973 and 1974, the Skylab spacecraft orbited Earth. Solar telescopes and cameras were positioned in the circular area at the centers of four windmill-like solar panels.

In 1984, space-suited astronaut George Nelson flew out to the Solar Maximum Mission satellite to capture it and bring it into the payload bay of the space shuttle for repairs.

The story of our Sun and the solar system began about 5 billion years ago. At that time, the Sun and its family of planets were nothing more than a huge cloud of gas and dust in the Milky Way galaxy.

Back on Earth, a movable mirror on the McMath Solar Telescope on Kitt Peak in Arizona bounces sunlight into a 500-foot (153-meter) tube to project a large image of the Sun.

Perhaps a nearby star exploded or a very dense star passed close by and caused the cloud to collapse. Because of gravity, the cloud of gas and dust collapsed into itself, and then began to rotate and flatten into a disk shape. Most of the gas and dust was at the center of the debris. Eventually pressure and temperatures increased, and fusion ignited this center cluster to form the Sun. Smaller clusters of dust and gas formed at varying distances from the center. These became the planets, comets, and asteroids.

The End

How long will the Sun last? Like all stars, the Sun will age and continue to change and will eventually vanish.

The fusion process inside the Sun converts about 4 million tons of matter to energy every second. In about 5 billion years, the Sun will have used up most of its hydrogen fuel. Eventually it will expand hundreds of times and become larger than the orbit of Earth. Then it will swallow up its solar system and become a *red giant* star. For a time, it will pulsate and shed shells of gas into space. The remains of the Sun will then condense into a tiny, very hot *white dwarf* star. Gradually, it will cool and become a dark cinder in space.

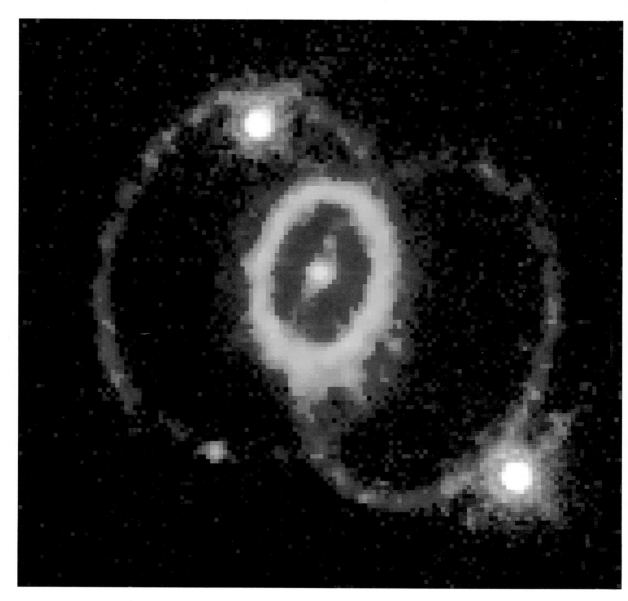

All stars have a natural life cycle. In 1987, a star in the Large Magellanic Cloud, a small galaxy beyond the Milky Way, exploded into a supernova. NASA's Hubble Space Telescope took this picture of the remnants of the star, which is called Supernova 1987A. Hubble Space Telescope pictures are made up of tiny squares, similar to those you see on the screen of a television set if you get very close to it. The two white dots are nearby stars.

This is a photograph of an annular solar eclipse over the Pacific Ocean, taken from the coast of San Diego, California. An annular eclipse occurs when the Moon passes in front of the Sun but does not cover the Sun entirely. During the eclipse, the Sun's atmosphere becomes visible.

The end of our Sun is hard to imagine, but it isn't something to worry about. The Sun will be with us for several billions of years more!

SUN QUICK FACTS

Sun: Known to ancient Romans as *Sol* and to ancient Greeks as *Helios*.

Average distance from Earth
    Millions of miles   93
    Millions of kilometers   149.6

Rotation (spinning once at its   27 days
equator. Rotation rate varies
with latitude.)

Diameter at Equator
    Miles   864,000
    Kilometers   1,390,000

Surface Gravity (compared to   28
Earth's)

Mass (the amount of matter   330,000
contained in the Sun compared
to Earth's)

Composition   Primarily hydrogen and helium

Atmosphere   Electrified gas (very thin)

Satellites   9 planets, 63 moons, trillions of
                                    comets, asteroids, and meteors

GLOSSARY

Atmosphere	The collection of gases that surround a planet.
Aurora	Glowing ribbons or curtains of light that appear in the northern or southern night sky when electrically charged particles from the Sun interact with gas in the upper atmosphere of Earth.
Chromosphere	The colorful, innermost atmosphere layer of the Sun.
Corona	The outer atmosphere of the Sun.
Density	A measurement of an object that compares its volume with the amount of matter packed into it.
Flares	Powerful explosions from the Sun's surface that shoot electrified particles into space.
Fusion	A nuclear process in which hydrogen atoms are fused together to produce helium atoms and release energy.
Granules	Circular areas on the Sun's surface caused by hot material boiling up from the Sun's interior.
Gravity	A force that causes objects to attract each other.
Milky Way galaxy	The spiral galaxy of stars of which our Sun is a member.

Photosphere	The Sun's apparent surface.
Prominences	Flamelike activity on the Sun that creates huge arching ribbons reaching hundreds of thousands of miles above the surface.
Red giant	The stage in the life of a star when it has consumed its fuel and expanded hundreds of times.
Solar telescope	A telescope designed especially for studying the Sun.
Solar wind	High-speed streams of electrically charged particles traveling away from the Sun.
Spicules	Spike-shaped explosions reaching thousands of miles above the Sun's surface.
Star	A ball of glowing gas in space.
Sunspots	Magnetic storms in the Sun's surface that appear darker than the rest of the photosphere.
Supergranules	Giant granules.
White dwarf	The stage in the life of a star when it has collapsed into a small, brightly glowing core.

FOR FURTHER READING

Couper, Heather, and Henbest, Nigel. *The Sun.* Space Scientist series. New York: Franklin Watts, 1986.

Estalella, Robert. *Our Star: The Sun.* Window on the Universe series. Hauppauge, New York: Barron's Educational Service, 1993.

Gallant, Roy. *Our Universe.* Washington, D.C.: National Geographic Society, 1986.

Rathbun, Elizabeth. *Exploring Your Solar System.* Washington, D.C.: National Geographic Society, 1989.

————. *Astronomy.* Milwaukee: Raintree Publishers, 1988.

INDEX

Page numbers in *italics* refer to illustrations.

Sun
    atmosphere of, 6, 9, 14-16, 26
    auroras and, 18, *19*
    beginning of, 18, 21, 23
    chromosphere of, 15, 16
    composition of, 6, 8-9, 26
    corona of, *15,* 15-16, *17,* 18
    density of, 8, 16
    diameter of, 6, 26
    distance to Earth, 5, 26
    eclipses and, 14, *14, 25*
    end of, 23, 25
    flares and, 12, *12, 13*
    granules of, 9-10
    gravity and, 5, 8, 26
    mass of, 26

Sun (*continued*)
    photosphere of, 9, 15, 16
    prominences and, *12,* 12-14
    rotation of, 26
    solar wind and, 18, 19
    spicules and, 12
    sunspots of, *10,* 10-11, *11*
Sunspots, *10,* 10-11, *11*
Supergranules, 10
Supernova 1987A, *24*

Temperature, 8

White dwarf star, 23

Yohkoh satellite, *7, 10*

ABOUT THE AUTHOR

Gregory L. Vogt works for NASA's Education Division at the Johnson Space Center in Houston, Texas. He works with astronauts in developing educational videos for schools.

Mr. Vogt previously served as the executive director of the Discovery World Museum of Science, Economics and Technology in Milwaukee, Wisconsin, and as an eighth-grade science teacher. He holds bachelor's and master's degrees in science from the University of Wisconsin at Milwaukee, as well as a doctorate in curriculum and instruction from Oklahoma State University.